Henry Ford
and the Model T Car

by Monica L. Rausch

Reading consultant: Susan Nations, M.Ed.,
author/literacy coach/consultant
in literacy development

Science and curriculum consultant:
Debra Voege, M.A., science and math curriculum
resource teacher

WEEKLY READER®
PUBLISHING

Please visit our web site at: www.garethstevens.com
For a free color catalog describing our list of high-quality books,
call 1-800-542-2595 (USA) or 1-800-387-3178 (Canada).
Our fax: 1-877-542-2596.

Library of Congress Cataloging-in-Publication Data

Rausch, Monica.
  Henry Ford and the Model T car / by Monica L. Rausch.
    p. cm. — (Inventors and their discoveries)
  Includes bibliographical references and index.
  ISBN-13: 978-0-8368-7500-3 (lib. bdg.)
  ISBN-13: 978-0-8368-7731-1 (softcover)
  1. Ford, Henry, 1863-1947—Juvenile literature. 2. Automobile engineers—United States—Biography—Juvenile literature.
  3. Inventors—United States—Biography—Juvenile literature. 4. Ford Model T automobile—Juvenile literature. I. Title.
TL140.F6R38   2007
629.222092—dc22
                                              2006029998

This edition first published in 2007 by
Weekly Reader® Books
An Imprint of Gareth Stevens Publishing
1 Reader's Digest Road
Pleasantville, NY 10570-7000 USA

Copyright © 2007 by Weekly Reader® Early Learning Library

Editor: Dorothy L. Gibbs
Cover design and page layout: Kami Strunsee
Picture research: Sabrina Crewe

Picture credits: cover (main), pp. 4, 7, 8, 10, 12, 20 The Granger Collection, New York; cover (right), title page
Library of Congress; pp. 5, 6, 9 © North Wind Picture Archives; p. 11 © Corbis; pp. 13 (both), 14, 15, 16, 17, 19, 21
© Bettmann/Corbis; p. 18 © Underwood & Underwood/Corbis.

Printed in the United States of America

2 3 4 5 6 7 8 9 10 10 09 08

Table of Contents

Cover: The 1908 Model T had a different body style than other Model Ts, but the engines in all Model T cars were the same.

Cover and title page: Henry Ford (1863–1947) started the Ford Motor Company in 1903.

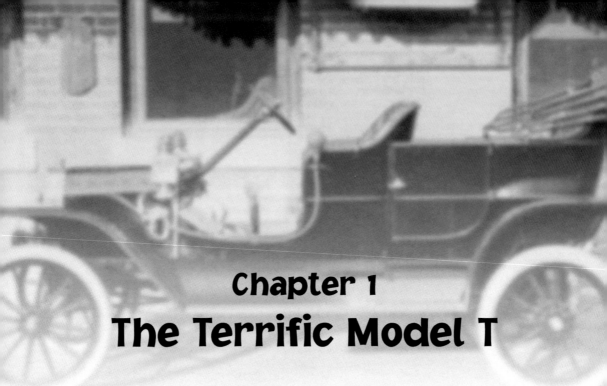

Chapter 1
The Terrific Model T

A shiny new **automobile**, or car, rolled out of the Ford
factory in Detroit, Michigan. It was October 1, 1908.
The first Model T was on its way to its new owner.

The Model T was not a heavy car, but it was strong. It was strong enough to travel on bumpy dirt roads. It was made out of a new kind of steel. The Model T was easy to drive, too. It had few parts and a simple **design**. If a Model T broke down, a person could fix it very easily.

In the early 1900s, roads were very bumpy. They were made for horses and wagons, not for cars.

Henry Ford was proud of the Model T. He had worked for two years planning the design of his new car — but he was not done yet! Ford wanted to build the Model T more quickly and for less money. He wanted everyone to be able to buy a Model T.

At first, only people with a lot of money could buy cars. This steam-powered automobile from 1907 was thought of as a "gentleman's car."

The Ford Model T cost $850 in 1908. By the 1920s, it cost less than $300 so many more people were buying Model Ts to drive to work.

Over the next five years, Ford worked to find a better way to build Model Ts. By 1914, his cars were being made very quickly and at a very low cost. Many more people could **afford** to buy them. The Model T was changing the way people in the United States traveled!

Chapter 2
From the Farm to the Factory

Henry Ford was born on July 20, 1863, in Dearborn, Michigan. When he was young, he liked to play with toys that had moving parts. His younger sisters and brothers had to keep their toys away from Henry. He would take them apart to see how they worked!

When Ford was about thirteen years old, he saw a farm wagon that moved without horses pulling it. The wagon used a **steam engine** to make it move. Ford was amazed. He asked the farmer to tell him all about how the wagon worked.

In the late 1800s, some farmers used wagons and tractors with steam engines. These engines were very expensive, and they were hard to start.

Henry Ford and his son Edsel are looking at a machine on display in New York in 1928. It is a turning machine called a lathe (laythe). It is Ford's first lathe. Ford used this machine in 1894 in his small workshop in Detroit.

Ford could not forget that amazing machine. At age sixteen, he left his father's farm to work on machines in Detroit, Michigan. He dreamed of building a new machine. Ford's father wanted him to run a farm, but Ford did not want to give up on his dream.

Before the 1900s, most people traveled from place to place in wagons or **carriages** that were pulled by horses. Ford wanted to build a carriage people could travel in without needing horses to pull it. Ford wanted to build a "horseless carriage."

In 1897, some large cities had electric streetcars, but city streets were still filled with horses and carriages.

11

Chapter 3
Everyone's Car

Henry Ford was not the first person, or the only person, who wanted to build a "horseless carriage." Some people built carriages that used steam engines to move. A steam engine was very heavy, and, sometimes, when the steam got too hot, the engine exploded!

A car with a steam engine needed water to run. The water was heated in the engine to make steam. The steam made the power to move the car.

Electric Car (1890s)

Other people built carriages with electric engines. These engines ran on **batteries**. A carriage with an electric engine could not move very fast, and it did not run very long before the battery ran out of power.

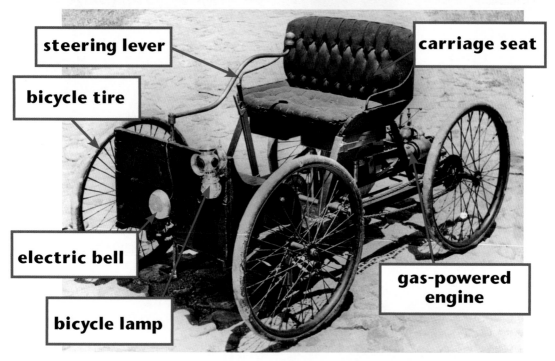

steering lever

carriage seat

bicycle tire

electric bell

gas-powered engine

bicycle lamp

Ford built his first car using parts of other vehicles. The car's gasoline engine was behind the seat.

Ford believed that a gasoline engine was the best kind to use on a horseless carriage. In 1896, Ford used a gasoline engine to power his first automobile. The car had a top speed of 20 miles (32 kilometers) per hour.

The first cars cost a lot to make. They were made one at a time. Every car was a little bit different, and no car was made exactly the same each time. Because cars cost so much and did not move very fast, most people did not think they were useful.

This 1902 car moved at only about 14 miles (23 km) per hour. It took seven and a half days to drive the car from Detroit to an auto show in New York.

Ford made this race car in 1902. It traveled at 60 miles (97 km) per hour. It set a United States record for speed.

In 1902, Ford built a race car. He thought that if he made a fast car, people would start to believe cars were useful. His race car amazed people. Ford was finally ready to build cars everyone could use.

Ford tried making many different **models** of cars, starting with the Model A. He worked hard to make a useful car that did not cost very much. That car was the Model T. Next, Ford needed to build good cars more quickly. In 1913, he found a way.

Ford finished the design for the Model T in 1908. It had a gasoline engine in front, with a cover, or hood, over it. A hand crank started the engine.

windshield

wooden steering wheel

covered engine

side oil lamp

hand crank

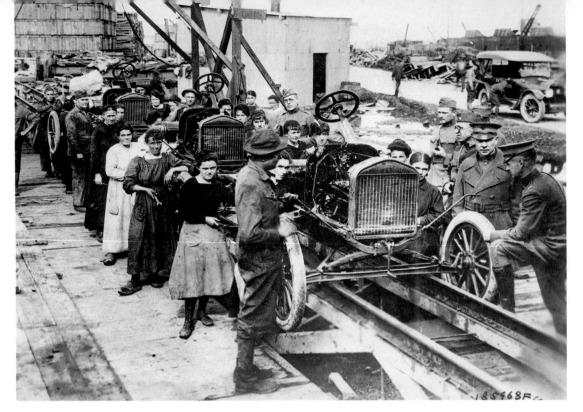

On an assembly line, every car was made with exactly the same parts. Each car was not made special or different.

In 1913, the workers at Ford's factory started building cars a new way. They started working on an **assembly line**. The workers stood in two lines, and the cars moved along a track or on a rolling belt between them.

When the rolling belt stopped, the workers at that place on the line would each do one special task to help build a car. Each worker did not have to know how to build the whole car. Each worker only needed to know how to do one task.

Workers on this 1913 assembly line are making only one kind of car part. On an assembly line, the time it took to make the part dropped from twenty minutes to five minutes.

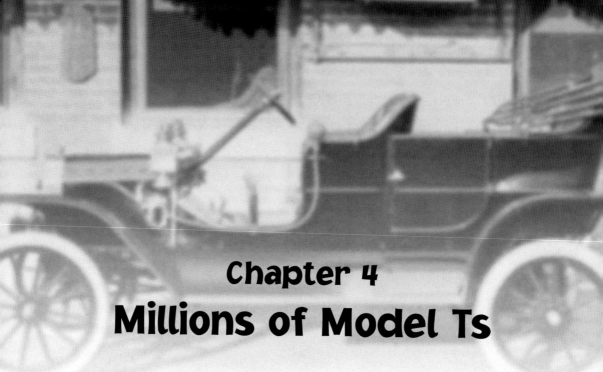

Chapter 4
Millions of Model Ts

Ford workers finished the first Model T in October 1908. During that month, they made only ten more Model Ts. In December 1908, however, Henry Ford's factory made two hundred Model Ts! As workers made the cars faster and faster, the price dropped lower and lower.

A Model T once took more than twelve hours to build. By 1914, workers could build a Model T in one hour and thirty-three minutes! Ford made cars faster than any other car company, and more and more people bought Model Ts. By 1924, more than ten million Model Ts had been sold. Everyone wanted a Ford Model T!

Henry Ford sits proudly in one of his automobiles in front of his company's factory in the 1920's.

Glossary

afford — to have enough money to buy something

assembly line — a line of workers that each stay in one place while the objects they are making, or assembling, move from person to person

automobile — a machine with wheels that carries people from place to place, using an engine to make it move; a car

carriages — enclosed wheeled vehicles that are usually pulled by horses and that have seats inside for passengers

design — (n) a plan or a pattern for building something

lathe — a machine tool used to cut metal into cylinder shapes

models — objects that are made from designs and are used as patterns to make more objects just like them

Books

Eat My Dust! Henry Ford's First Race. Step into Reading (series). Monica Kulling (Random House)

Henry Ford. Rookie Biographies (series). Wil Mara (Children's Press)

Henry Ford: The Car Man. Famous Inventors (series). Carin T. Ford (Enslow Elementary)

Henry Ford: A Photo-Illustrated Biography. Photo-Illustrated Biographies (series). Erika L. Shores (Bridgestone Books)

The Story of Model T Fords. Classic Cars (series). David K. Wright (Gareth Stevens)

Web Site

Model T Road Trip
www.thehenryford.org/exhibits/smartfun/welcome.html
Join a family that buys a Model T and takes a trip in 1919.

Publisher's note to educators and parents: Our editors have carefully reviewed this Web site to ensure that it is suitable for children. Many Web sites change frequently, however, and we cannot guarantee that a site's future contents will continue to meet our high standards of quality and educational value. Be advised that children should be closely supervised whenever they access the Internet.

Index

About the Author

Monica L. Rausch has a master's degree in creative writing from the University of Wisconsin-Milwaukee, where she is currently teaching composition, literature, and creative writing. Monica likes to write fiction, but she says sticking to the facts is fun, too. Monica lives in Milwaukee near her six nieces and nephews, to whom she loves to read books.